A Holliston Call to Duty

To my favorite Cousen
Mary Nolan
Remember
July 19/21
Bobby Blair

BOBBY BLAIR
The "Mayor of Mudville"

A Holliston Call to Duty

Text and cover photo © Bobby Blair

Designer/Art Director – LisaThompsonGraphicDesign.com
Editor – PeruzziCommunications.com

Library of Congress Control Number: 2021905198
ISBN: 9781941573259

Published by Damianos Publishing
Saxonville Mills
2 Central Street, Studio 152
Framingham, MA 01701
www.DamianosPublishing.com

Produced through Silver Street Media by Bridgeport National Bindery, Agawam, MA USA

First printed 2021

About the Photos

In 1973 as the historian for American Legion Post 47, I began collecting photos of past commanders along with activities at the post. The hobby branched out over the years to include all veterans regardless of affiliation in town. The collection of photos grew over the years. Most were given by friends and relatives, and many I snapped myself. For this book I enlisted the help of the Holliston Historical Society. To all those who contributed, thank you for the future generations in town who can learn a little bit about the previous and present veterans in their home town.

Everett Blair served in the US Navy during World War II

Dedication

This book is dedicated to my dad, Everett Blair, who served in the US Navy during World War II. One of six brothers who entered military service, dad rose to the rank of chief petty officer aboard the *USS Hailey* (DD-556), earning six battle stars. The *USS Hailey* would see action at the battles of Kwajalein Atoll, Eniwetok, New Guinea, Marianos, Leyte Gulf, Okinawa and Formosa. Dad was a charter member of the local VFW Post 8507 and a past commander of the American Legion Post 47. Dad would instill a sense of patriotism in his five children, his three sons Robert and Michael serving in Vietnam and the youngest, Thomas, serving aboard the *USS Saratoga*. Right up until his passing at ninety-two years of age, dad never missed participating in a local Memorial Day parade in sixty-six years.

Introduction

Can you list the names of ten military veterans from Holliston, living or dead? Little has been told much less published about the lives of Holliston's men and women who were called in times of peace and war to the nation's defense. No collection of photographs of this town's veterans has ever been assembled under one cover for the posterity of future generations.

In the following pages, I hope to give you the reader a small glimpse of Holliston residents through images of those who answered their nation's call to serve. "All gave some, some gave all". There are no photos of those from town who served in the French and Indian War, nor of the town's Minutemen who marched towards Roxbury on April 19, 1775; the camera simply had not yet been invented. Our book of images begins with the Civil War of 1861 to 1865, from that new device called a camera.

Hailing from a family of Massachusetts citizen soldiers that traces its service back to Lexington and Concord and Bunker Hill I've always yearned to learn more about my family's military history. Relative Henry Lewis Stimson would serve under Presidents Taft, Hoover, and Roosevelt as Secretary of War. My paternal grandmother Marjorie (Stimpson) Blair would lose her brother George Stimpson in World War I when he was killed in action in France. During World War II Nana sent off her six sons for duty with Uncle Sam. My maternal grandfather Jerome Moore would see service in France during World War I, then see his three sons enter military service beginning in World War II. As a half-century member of the local American Legion and

VFW, I spearheaded the arrival of the Vietnam "Moving Wall" during the town's 275th Anniversary in 1999, and later the writing and placing of posters on utility poles listing the rank, name, age, and state of those killed in Iraq and Afghanistan since 2003. These projects have given me a unique view of the sacrifices of war.

The photographs in the book may be of a familiar place you know, or former neighbor, or a relative. The veterans in the book may revive a long-lost story that was handed down by word of mouth. While I have procrastinated for many years to begin a book, it was in 2006 that I realized there was no known photo of a group of the town's World War II veterans. With a selfish scheme in mind to get a group photo, I suggested a dinner for veterans on Veterans Day at town hall. With the help of the local American Legion, VFW, and Lions Club, the photograph was captured, and the tradition of the annual dinner lives on.

Hopefully, this book, whether a keepsake for yourself or as a gift to someone, will inspire others to record history. When it comes to hard copy photographs, always print the name, date, and location of those captured in the photo on the reverse side of the photo. While I've tried to record as many names in the book as possible, those of an older vintage proved difficult as no one alive can identify them. The book captures but a small segment of the town's veteran population, living and dead, and a second edition may be required in the near future.

As this book is of a local nature, only a limited number will be printed. Now about you trying to list the names of ten Holliston veterans: Read on, I'll help you out!

A sign located near Adams Street and Gorwin Drive

While no photos exist of Holliston men in the Revolutionary War, it would be remiss in not mentioning Paul Revere's connection to Holliston. In his diary, Timothy Dickinson wrote of a visit to Holliston from Dr. Richardson and Paul Revere in 1795. Revere revealed the incidents of April 19, 1775 and Dickinson said that "Revere had a connection to Holliston during the Revolution".

In the Holliston Assessors list of 1775, Paul Revere was taxed, one poll, no real estate and two in personal property. Noted local historian Dan Chase writes that Revere lived on Adams Street near Underwood Street (presently Gorwin Drive) in a house between the homes of Leland and Bridges. "I believe signs of a cellar hole and a well were there at that time," Chase noted. He admitted that he doesn't know why Revere wanted his family here or how he became acquainted with Holliston.

Resting place of Staples Chamberlain at Paddy Lincoln's Cemetery on Gorwin Drive

Capt. Staples Chamberlain's efforts towards America's independence are remarkable if not heroic. Taking part in the siege of Fort Ticonderoga, Chamberlain would answer the call on April 19, 1775, marching to Roxbury. A later expedition saw Chamberlain heading up a company of men for a suspected British attack on Newport, Rhode Island in 1780. At a town meeting on January 13, 1778, it was voted to send Holliston men in the Continental Army a shirt, breeches, one pair of shoes, and stockings. Late in January, Chamberlain, the town moderator and a man of fifty years, set out in deep snow on horse and wagon across the Berkshires and arrived in Albany, New York on February 6. Leaving supplies for eight Holliston men, Chamberlain headed to Valley Forge next to deliver the rest of his cargo. Heading home, Chamberlain would make it in time to moderate the annual town meeting in early March.

*Members of Holliston's Post 6 GAR (Grand Army of
the Republic) in the town square*

While no battlefield photos of Holliston's Company B, Sixteenth Regiment are known to exist, this photo may be the earliest known photo of Holliston's Civil War veterans. The date is unknown. The only named person in the photo is Patrick Finn, second from the right.

Benjamin Hamlet is buried in the center rear of the
Central Burial Ground next to town hall

Benjamin

He lieth in a grave in town
His stone immersed beneath the ground,
A tree drapes dead across his plot,
Have we forgotten the battles he's fought?

Though Holliston was his abode.
He came from Dracut, not far down the road,
Joined General Butler's Company "C",
30th Regiment, a private you see.

Deep in the South, New Orleans we're told,
Malarial sickness began to take hold,
Himself a victim, he suffered the strain,
Mustered in '62 he enlisted again.

Fought for the Union, a wound in his side,
His bravery at Cedar Creek fills me with pride,
This man I knew not, but wish I had,
Too many years between him and my dad.

The rebellion is over, it's time to withdraw,
Only the living have gained from the war,
Comrades lie many, all over the land,
The men you walked with on a given command.

I stand before your humble place,
And feel the pride drip down my face,
It's me grandfather! I carry your name,
No battle on earth shall displace that claim!

Shirley (Hamlet) Chipman
1997

John Plympton

John Plympton, a Medfield resident, would join Holliston's
Company B on July 12, 1861. A private, Plympton would see an
extra stripe added to his sleeve in September 1863, rising to the
rank of corporal. Plympton took part in all of Company B's major
battles including Fair Oaks, Fredericksburg and Gettysburg.
Plympton would re-enlist in 1864 to the Eleventh Infantry
Company E and finally be discharged in July 1865 near
Alexandria, Virginia.

William Harrison Austin

William Austin, a member of Post 6 GAR, entered the service at East Brookfield, Massachusetts as a corporal in the Twenty-fourth Massachusetts Infantry in September 1861. Austin took part in a number of battles including a march to Goldsboro under Gen. J. G. Foster to burn the salt works at Swansboro, North Carolina. Austin wrote in the GAR Historical Records, "While on picket duty at Seabrook Island S.C. I became sick with chill and fever from which I have never fully recovered."

Benjamin A. Bridges

Benjamin Bridges entered into service on July 2, 1861 with the rank of first sergeant. A member of Holliston's Company B, Bridges attained the rank of second lieutenant in August of 1862, first lieutenant in November of 1862, and captain on July 19, 1863. Wounded in action at Chancellorsville on May 3, 1863, Bridges was discharged on November 3 for disability at Washington, D.C. The local Sons of Veterans Camp 63 was named in Bridges' honor.

Otis J. Andrews

Otis Andrews entered the military from Holliston on August 13, 1862 as a private. He was assigned to Company K, Thirty-eighth Regiment, Massachusetts Volunteers, 19 Army Corps. He participated in a number of engagements including Fisher's Kill and Cedar Creek in 1863. Andrews' most vivid memories of the war were burying the dead at Port Hudson on June 17, 1863. Andrews died on February 23, 1918 at his Front Street home and is buried at Lake Grove Cemetery.

Granville Leland

Granville Leland was born in Holliston on July 7, 1827. Leland's first battle was at Fair Oaks in June of 1862. The Fair Oaks Campaign would be Holliston's worst toll of the entire Civil War. Three were killed, four wounded and one taken prisoner. Leland would serve out his enlistment and was discharged on July 27, 1864.

Althamer Chamberlain on the left and G.R. Russell

Two of the town's last living Civil War veterans pose for the camera. Althamer Chamberlain was a Central Street resident and G.R. Russell owned a grocery and dry goods store at 101 Central Street. G.R.'s store was torn down in 1959 and a new building erected by G.R.'s son-in-law Freddie Cole.

The new building, a supermarket, was known as Russell's. The building was later purchased by CVS Pharmacy.

Edwin Day Pond

Edwin Pond would serve with the Forty-second Regiment of the Massachusetts Infantry, Company B. Like many of his fellow soldiers, Pond suffered from malaria and chronic diarrhea. The steamer carrying Pond home ran aground in heavy fog at Point Judith. Attempting to reach a rope ladder on the *City of Newport,* Pond was thrown against the ship, causing injury. When his first wife died and his only son didn't make it to adulthood, Pond remarried and had two children. Pond lived at 28 Franklin Street. As his health declined, they rented out rooms to supplement their income. He died in 1903 at age 67.

GAR Post 6 members in front of their quarters at
21 Green Street

Front row from left, Daniel Travis, unknown, Alexander B. French, John Noble Fiske, Otis Andrews, Henry H. Belcher, Thomas Galligan, John Howarth, John Collins, Albert Wiley, and Robert H. Griffen. Second row from left, Frank Sager, William H. Austin, Edward Pond, John Littlefield, O. L. Cutting, G. R. Russell, William H. Clark, unknown, Benjamin A. Bridges, Granville Leland, J. S. Simmons, unknown. On steps from left, John H. Hart, Althamer Chamberlain, William H. Burch, and Lewis H. Bullard.

John Mellen Payson

John Mellon Payson was part of Holliston Company B's fight at
Fair Oaks and the Seven Days Fight in 1862. He became sick
with kidney and liver troubles according to his orderly sergeant.
During the Battle of the Wilderness in 1864, Payson was in
charge of five of the officer's horses. The horses became
unmanageable, dragging him from his saddle and over the head
of the horse he was riding, and he was thrown to the ground
with great violence. Married twice, his first wife died when the
youngest of three girls was two. He remarried. Payson lived at
the corner of Union and Central Streets where he operated a
stable. He later worked as a mason and contractor. He lived to be
89 years of age.

*GAR Building on Exchange Street at the turn of the
twentieth century*

Built in 1878, the building was the first to be owned and occupied by a GAR Post in Massachusetts. The land being leased at 21 Green Street, the post purchased land at 13 Exchange Street and moved the building in two pieces. With the advancing age of Civil War veterans, the GAR sold the building to the Sons of Vets Camp 63 on July 18, 1918. Meeting at town hall and eventually at the GAR building, the local American Legion Post 47 purchased the building on January 23, 1941. The American Legion would sell the property in 1999 and hold their meetings in a small meeting room held by the local VFW located on Woodland Street.

John Hart

GAR Post 6 member John Hart entered the military on August
22, 1861 at Baltimore, Maryland. As part of Holliston's Company
B, Hart's military service would be short-lived because of a
disability he received at the skirmish at Glendale. The
engagements were also known as the Battle of Frayser's Farm or
the Seven Day Battles. Hart was discharged on December 15,
1862.

Jeremiah S. Simmons

Jeremiah S. Simmons was a member of GAR Post 6. He enlisted to Company A, Thirty-first Massachusetts Volunteers Infantry, on November 9, 1861 at Pittsfield. Attaining the rank of sergeant, Simmons was discharged after the taking of New Orleans under Gen. G. F. Butler, where he was injured on May 1, 1862.

Sgt. Silas Cobb's gravestone is located in the Central Burial Ground

Silas Cobb, a Holliston bootmaker, entered the military on July 13, 1863 as a corporal in Company F, Third Massachusetts Heavy Artillery. After Cobb's infamous brush with history and rising to the rank of sergeant, he was discharged in September of 1865. At the age of 29, Cobb along with three others drowned in a boating mishap in Grand Haven, Michigan. Edgar Fletcher of Holliston also lost his life in the incident.

*Holliston's Civil War
Monument*

Albert Darling came to reside in Holliston after the war and was a member of Post 6, GAR. On April 16, 1861, the nineteen-year-old enlisted in the Third Regiment, Massachusetts Volunteers. Discharged on July 22, Darling reenlisted to the Eighteenth Massachusetts Volunteers on September 17, 1861. Discharged again in April 1864, Darling reenlisted to the Ninth Regiment Veterans Reserve Corps on April 9, 1864 and was discharged for the last time on November 25, 1865. Darling saw action at the battles of Bull Run, Fredericksburg, and Gettysburg. A witness to history, Darling was at Ford's Theatre the night President Lincoln was shot. Darling also had the honor of carrying the flag at Lincoln's funeral, and "saw the prisoners hung for the assassination of the president, being on duty there at that time."

GAR Post 6 members mount the steps at town hall

Aging members of GAR Post 6 climb the steps at town hall during a Memorial Day ceremony. Members of Camp 63 Sons of Vets act as an honor guard. Note Elm Street in the background is still a dirt road.

*Walter Moynihan, first commander of American Legion
Post 47*

Local lore has it that when the town's newly minted doughboys arrived to take part in the Annual Memorial Day Parade in 1920, Comdr. Walter Moynihan and his American Legion group were directed by Post 6 GAR members as to their position in the line of march. The Civil War veterans had run the parade for the past forty years. The World War I veterans were incensed to find out that the Civil War veterans had placed them dead last in the line of march behind the younger scouts in town. When sensible heads failed to prevail, Moynihan ordered his contingent to form a separate parade. The two parades passed each other in the town center, and it was the last time Holliston ever had two parades on Memorial Day.

Charlie Williams

World War I veteran Charlie Williams owned and operated Williams Market at the corner of Central and Washington Streets. Williams employed fellow World War I veteran Walter Higgins as his sidekick. A charter member of the town's Lions Club, Williams was the "news gleaner" for the Lions Club's *Holliston Servicemen's News* during World War II.

William Sheehan

William Sheehan of Green Street saw his first military service with the Irish Fusiliers in World War I. Upon the entry of the United States in that war, Sheehan transferred into the US Navy. In May of 1942, Sheehan was sworn in for special service in the First Naval District, becoming one of the few known men in town to serve in both world wars.

*World War I veterans parade through the town center
during their welcome home celebration in 1919*

Four Holliston men died in the military during World War I –
Harold Gallison, Ernest Kehoe, Charles Duford, and James
Cutler. Hollistonians jumped the gun when it came time to
celebrate, however. While a truce was not enacted until
November 11, 1918, townspeople began celebrating in
compliance with Gov. McCall's proclamation of July 20, 1918.
"Holliston last evening observed the Allies victory in France by
ringing church bells and blowing of factory horns and fire alarm
gongs." The streets were thronged with sightseers and cheering
crowds. A bonfire was held in the town square, with the singing
of the Star-Spangled Banner and rousing cheers for the boys over
there.

Leo F. Clancy

Leo Clancy, a 1910 graduate of Holliston High, went on to graduate from Jefferson Medical College, before setting up a medical practice in Ennis, Montana. Returning east to complete his military service, Clancy would practice medicine from his 918 Washington Street home and leave a legacy as Holliston's last country doctor who made house calls.

Ernest G. Kehoe

Ernest Kehoe was educated in Holliston schools and was employed as a shoe cutter. Serving in the US Army, Kehoe saw service in Panama and the Mexican border before being assigned to the Thirty-eighth Regiment, Third Infantry Division, 101 Machine Gun Company. During the last German drive in France, Kehoe was killed in action on July 5, 1918. The son of Mr. and Mrs. Horace Kehoe, who had predeceased the twenty-three-year-old soldier, Kehoe lived with his Drennan family relatives at 32 Arch Street. Kehoe is buried at the Anise-Marne American Cemetery in Belleau, France.

Harold Lang

Serving in the US Navy during World War I, Harold Lang would serve as a commander for the local Legion Post 47. When the American Legion purchased their building at 13 Exchange Street from the Sons of Vets, Lang became a trustee of the Holliston Veterans Building Association. Employed by the Draper Corporation in Hopedale, Lang was a long-time volunteer of the town's fire department. Lang's son Walter erected greenhouses on their Avon Street properties where the family grew springtime flowers and vegetables for the locals.

Jerome Moore

Jerome Moore was born in Antigonish, Nova Scotia and moved to his School Street home in the late 1890s. Serving with an Army Transportation Company in France, Moore would return to help his father Louis run the family business, Moore Monumental, in the backyard of their 45 School Street home. Moore married his 61 School Street neighbor Mary Driscoll and the couple raised their five children at 22 School Street. Moore served as the town's assistant fire chief.

Charles F. Duford

Charles F. Duford would become what was believed at that time to be Holliston's first casualty during World War I. A member of the Army's Company M, 326th Infantry Regiment, Eighty-second Infantry Division, Sgt. Duford was killed in action in the Argonne Forest of France on October 14, 1918. He is buried in the Meuse-Argonne American Cemetery in Romagne, France. The local American Legion Post 47 is named in Duford's honor. Ernest Kehoe actually was killed in action two months prior to Duford and overlooked by the town – his name not appearing on the town's veterans honor roll at town hall. He was honored by the Legion Post in 2003 with a square dedicated in his name at Arch and Water Streets.

American Legion Post 47 marches their colors through the town center, circa 1939

The American Legion Color Guard marches through the town square past the Economy Grocery Stores (present day Holliston Superette). Pictured in the center is Jerome Moore, a charter member of the Legion post and one of the adult leaders of the post's Drum and Bugle Corps. To Moore's right is Harold (Pappy) Shea, who would serve the town as a selectman.

George Sherman

George Sherman, a Braggville resident, was Holliston's last
World War I veteran to pass away. A private first class in the
Army, Sherman served as an engineer in the boiler room at
Camp Devens. Born December 31, 1894, Sherman died 58 days
short of his one hundredth birthday on November 13, 1994.

*American Legion Post 47 Junior Drum and
Bugle Corps, circa 1936-37*

First row from left, Jerome Scanlon, Robert J. Moore, Bob Weston, Vin Mullen, John Mullen, Henry Beltrame, Nancy O'Grady, Helen Moore, Ellen O'Grady, Keith Donnelly, Arthur Parks, Warren Pidgeon, Bob Tweedie, Bill Clancy, Charles Maguire. Second row from left, Ted Barrett, Jerry Littlefield, Ralph Chapin, Henry Carr, Bob Taylor, John Clancy, Dick Locke, Wilbur Merritt, Jack Honey, Ray Chapin, Donald White, Stetson Avery. Back row from left, Bobby Fagan, Paul Maeder, Allen Bailey, Jack Locke, John Driscoll, John Adams, Billy Feehely, Bill Sheehan, and Paul Elder.

Note: Many of these musicians would enter military service during World War II.

Holliston's early wooden honor roll, circa 1942-43

The World War II honor roll as it stood in front of town hall around 1942-43. Constructed by Highway Superintendent Louis (Buck) Moore, the names were still being added as they weren't alphabetically listed . Note the high school in the mid-left of the photo.

Leonard D. Chesmore

Leonard D. Chesmore was an aviation radioman second class in the US Navy, a 1938 graduate of Holliston High School, and a member of the school's basketball team. Chesmore's plane was shot down over Tarawa in the South Pacific on December 24, 1943. The local VFW Post, 8507, is named in Chesmore's honor. Chesmore's body was never recovered.

Harold Kampersal

Harold Kampersal's unit, the Forty-fifth Infantry Division, had just crossed the Rhine and was heading towards the Battle of the Bulge. When his buddies were able to kill a few chickens, Kampersal searched an abandoned house for a frying pan to cook the chickens in. Finding a pan in the basement Kampersal heard a noise behind a door only to find a German pointing a gun at him. As a medic, Kampersal carried no weapon and only the cast iron skillet to defend himself. The German lowered his weapon and placed his hand on Kampersal's red cross and said "comrade". The German needed medical attention and surrendered to Kampersal. In January of 1990 on Kampersal's passing the American Legion on Exchange Street lowered their flag to half-mast and also hung a cast iron frying pan from the lanyard.

Burleigh E. Curtis

Burleigh Curtis was the vice president of his class at Holliston
High School in 1939. A first lieutenant with the Army's
377th Squadron, 362nd Fighter Bomb Group, Curtis' P-47D
crashed on a dive-bombing mission near Briouze, France on
June 13, 1944. Curtis' remains were not discovered until 2018
and returned to the United States in 2019. A memorial service
for Curtis was held at the First Baptist Church in 2019 and
attended by family members and town veterans. His memorial
square is located at the corner of Elm Street and Irving Place.
Curtis is buried next to his parents in Windham, Maine.

Walter and Alex Rossini aboard ship in the South Pacific

All four sons of Joe and Genevieve (Ma) Rossini of East Holliston would see service during World War II. After the war, the four brothers, Walter, Alex, Albino, and John expanded their ice cream business into what would become Walter's Dairy. The East Holliston fixture known for its fried clams and baked Alaska would operate until its closing in 1985.

Standing on the left, Benjamin "Blackey" Blackmer

Serving with the Army in Europe, Maj. Benjamin Blackmer
would raise his family after the war on Wilkens Road, later
purchasing a home downtown at 851 Washington Street. One of
the town's most decorated veterans of World War II, Blackey
earned the Distinguished Service Cross, two Silver Stars, two
Bronze Stars, two Purple hearts, a Distinguished Unit Citation,
the Croix de Guerre, Combat Infantry Badge, and a Presidential
Unit Citation, amongst other awards. Blackey owned Holliston
Floor Covering.

Walter Paul

Adams Street resident Walter Paul served with Patton's Third Army in Europe during the Battle of the Bulge. The battle took place from December 16, 1944 to January 25, 1945. Americans suffered their worst casualties from a surprise attack on December 16, 1944, making it their worst loss of any operation during the war. Paul was wounded twice during the battle and awarded two Purple Hearts. After returning home, Paul owned an automotive garage in Framingham. Paul is buried at Bourne National Cemetery.

Charles W. Lovewell

A graduate of Holliston High in the Class of 1934, Lt. Charles Lovewell would be married for only a brief time prior to his death. A member of the Army Air Forces 729th Bomber Squadron, 452nd Bomber Group, Lovewell's B-17 crashed on April 21, 1944 on a training mission. As a bombardier, Lovewell's position in the underneath of the plane left him vulnerable. The rest of the crew survived the crash. Lovewell is buried at Cambridge American Cemetery in Cambridge, England.

Louis P. Paltrineri

Joining the Army Air Corps on his eighteenth birthday,
Paltrineri, a radio operator, would fly thirty missions in his B-17
out of Thorpe Abbots, England before being shot down over
Germany. A prisoner of war at Stalag Luft 4, Gross-Tychow,
Paltrineri's camp was liberated in 1945. Paltrineri was
awarded a Distinguished Flying Cross, two Purple Hearts and
the Air Medal among other awards. He purchased Fiske's
General Store in 1973, and later was selected as Holliston's
Citizen of the Year in 1995.

William D. Kelley

A member of the 1939 Holliston High Basketball Team, Cpl. Kelley would be wounded in action during the invasion of Iwo Jima on February 23, 1945. Kelley died aboard a hospital ship and was buried at sea. Due to religious reasons, a memorial square was never erected for Kelley until 2003, when a surviving brother told the local American Legion enough time had passed since his brother's death. Kelley's memorial square is located near his childhood home on Rockland Street at the Bragg family cemetery.

Joseph D. Serocki

A private in the US Army's Fifteenth Infantry Regiment,
Third Infantry Division, Serocki was killed in action on
November 9, 1944. He is buried at Lorraine American Cemetery,
St. Arold, France. Serocki's memorial square is located on Rogers
Road near his childhood home.

Leonard T. Ryerson

While living at his family's poultry farm at 1797 Washington Street, Len Ryerson joined Britain's Royal Air Force via Canada in 1941. Transferring to America's Army Air Corps, Ryerson was killed on September 26, 1942 while his plane was escorting B-17s on a bombing run. The photo pictures Ryerson (upper right) as a member of RAF Squadron 133 with Winston Churchill. The undeveloped film was sent to Interstate Photo at 990 Washington Street and copies seemingly made it into every household in Holliston. Ryerson is buried at Brittany American Cemetery in St. James, France. Ryerson's memorial square is located at Washington Street and Johnson Drive.

Charlie Nickerson

While he may be better known as the former owner of Outpost Farm, Charlie Nickerson years earlier found himself jumping out of a plane on D-Day in 1944 as part of the Eighty-second Airborne Division. He earned two Silver Stars as well as a medal for valor from the Russians. As the lead reconnaissance scout for his unit, Nickerson would often find himself behind enemy lines. Nickerson would take part in the Battle of the Bulge and make his way with his unit to Berlin for the end of the war.

American Legion carnival

After the war, the local Legion Post held many town events.
Pictured at a carnival held at Goodwill Park are, from left,
Charles (Red) Chapin, a World War II POW, Ned Wise, Billy
Hamlet, Paul Mahoney, Ed Serocki, and "Hawk" Hayden. The
Legion Post was known as the biggest "little" post in the state
with over 400 members. Many of those members were
convalescing at Cushing Hospital in Framingham, where
servicemen were brought to recover.

VFW Post 8507

The Leonard D. Chesmore Post 8507 Veterans of Foreign Wars was organized on November 21, 1946. Members from the Spanish-American War, World War I, and World War II would complete the post's rolls after the first year, including eighteen original charter members. Edward Cox Jr. served as the first post commander. Meetings of the post were first held in lower town hall and then in the Cerel Building over Fiske's Store. In 1960, members began construction of new quarters on Woodland Street. Steel beams from the former Darling Woolen Mill, which burned down in 1934, were used in the construction of the new building. The building was sold in 2012 to a martial arts organization and the post meets in a small portion of the downstairs.

John Ghelli

John Ghelli landed at Inchon, Korea as part of the USMC's
First Marines, Seventh Motor Transport Battalion, Company C.
After the war, Ghelli would marry the girl next door, Wilma
Sherman. He worked for Rosenfeld Concrete for more than
thirty years. Ghelli was also a member of Braggville's volunteer
fire department.

Memorial Day, circa 1958-59

The American Legion colors are marched down Central Street past the Central Fire Station. From the left – George Mantell, Ernest (Alfie) Turner, Warren (Presty) Bresnahan, and Jimmy Blair. Legion Commander M. Vincent Connolly leads the contingent.

VFW Rifle Squad

Front row from left, Donald MacFarland, Francis Diani, Donald Drinkwater, Commander, George Lyden, Alton Moulton, Richard Pillotte, Richard Carpenter. Back row from left, Clifton Wheeler, Robert Smith, Frank Hancock, Kirmit Jones, Elwin Brown and Kenneth Williams.

Peter A. Holmberg

A Woodland Street resident and 1964 graduate of Holliston High School, Peter Holmberg was one of Holliston's most decorated soldiers during the Vietnam War. Holmberg served two tours in Vietnam with the Fifth Special Forces and II Corps Mobile Guerrilla Company. Holmberg was awarded two Silver Stars, four Bronze Stars, two Purple Hearts, four Army Commendation Medals with two "V" devices for valor, the Legion of Merit, the Soldiers Medal, the Vietnam Cross of Gallantry, among other numerous awards. Retiring as a sergeant major, Holmberg passed away on November 14, 2019 and is buried at Arlington National Cemetery.

Laura Hines

Winter Street resident Laura Hines was a student at Children's Hospital in Boston and in her final year of nursing school. An argument with her parents had Hines signing up in the Army after a recruiter happened by the hospital. One of nearly 5,000 women to serve in Vietnam, Hines would serve with the Sixty-seventh Evac Hospital in Qui Nhon. Hines seems to be sizing up this water buffalo in the photo.

Herb Brockert Jr.

Serving in the Central Highlands of Vietnam with B Company, First Battalion, Thirty-fifth Infantry, Third Brigade of the Twenty-fifth Infantry Division, Herb Brockert served as a radio operator. The owner of Construction Services, Brockert was selected as the town's Citizen of the Year in 2017. A long-time mentor for the Dedham Court House, Brockert helps veterans with treatment for addictions. Brockert was a huge proponent of the twenty-year effort to build the town's rail trail.

Thomas Ghelli

Thomas Ghelli, son of Francis and Betty (Kampersal), Ghelli would be one of three Holliston men to lose their lives in Vietnam. A member of A Company Third Battalion, Twenty-first Infantry, 196th Light Infantry Brigade, Ghelli was killed in action on January 10, 1968. His memorial stands at Goodwill Park and he is buried in Lake Grove Cemetery.

The American Legion Color Guard in 1974, the town's
250th anniversary

Front row from left — Bernie Blaney, Ernie Neilsen, Comdr. Bobby Blair, Tom Mahoney, and Harold Shea. Back row from left — Everett Blair, Bobby Ludwick and Jimmy Dalton.

The combined Color Guards of the VFW and American Legion march through the town center on the nation's bicentennial anniversary in 1976.

VFW Comdr. Bob Souther and Legion Comdr. Tom Hayes lead the contingent during the country's bicentennial year in 1976.

VFW Drill Squad

The VFW Drill Squad passes through the town center led by George Archambault and drummer Arthur (Sonny) Farnsworth. The longer march of Memorial Day parades to Lake Grove and St. Mary's cemeteries ended in the early 1960s when a selectman named Smith had a heart attack after the uphill climb of Phipp's Hill and passed away on Highland Street. The long route was only ever used again in 1985 when the town dedicated the honor roll of the town's Vietnam veterans.

*Vietnam Era veterans at the dedication of the Vietnam
Honor Roll at town hall, circa 1985*

From left — John Chartrand, Paul Chartrand, Ted Liscombe, Lloyd Davis, Joe Saulen, and Francis Hayes. World War II veteran Bob Higgins is looking on in the background.

Keith S. Napolitano

Pleasant Street resident Keith Napolitano would be deployed seven times to the Middle East and amass over 1,000 hours of combat flying time. Napolitano began his military career in 2002 as a second lieutenant. He is the holder of two Meritorious Service Medals, ten Air Medals, two Air Force Commendation Medals, an Air Force Combat Medal with a gold star, eight Outstanding Unit Awards, a Combat Readiness Medal, as well as many campaign medals. Lt. Col. Keith Napolitano is presently the commander of the 143rd Airlift Squadron out of Quonset Air National Guard Station in Rhode Island.

Eric Simkins

Arch Street and Mudville resident Eric Simkins enlisted in the Army in 2006, rising through the ranks from private to captain. With various duty stations in the US and Germany, Simkins would serve two tours of duty in Afghanistan and one in Iraq. Simkins is the holder of a Bronze Star, six Army Commendation Medals, four Army Achievement Medals, two NATO Medals, and a Meritorious Unit Award to name a few.

Michael Hamlet, right, along with his dad Darrell Hamlet,
a USMC veteran

Growing up on Winthrop Street, Michael Hamlet's Holliston military roots stretch back to the Civil War and his great-grandfather Benjamin Hamlet, who is buried in the Central Burial Ground. Master Sgt. Hamlet, an Air Force Reserve veteran, did five tours of the Middle East beginning just after 9/11, to Saudi Arabia, and other tours to Iraq and Afghanistan. Hamlet retired from the Holliston Post Office in 2021.

Peter Hill and Dan Valovcin

Sgt. First Class Peter Hill on the left, and Spc. Dan Valovcin were able to meet in Baghdad, Iraq in 2008 thanks to Facebook. Hill was a member of the 126th Forward Logistics Element and Valovcin was with an Army MP unit. Both would coincidentally serve on the Holliston Fire Department after their military service.

Veterans march past Hollis Street during a
Memorial Day Parade

James Hamm leads a contingent of veterans on Memorial Day. Hamm's maternal side of his family, the Finns, have a long Holliston history of serving in wars going back to his great-great-grandfather Patrick Finn, who served in the Civil War. Hamm, who served two tours in Iraq, is followed by Bill French, commander of the VFW in the line of march.

John Benda

John Benda graduated from Dedham High in 1997 and was
commissioned as an ensign in the US Navy in 2001. Assigned to
the *USS Ashlandem* in 2003 as part of Operation Iraqi Freedom,
Benda would also see service in the Far East and serve as an
operations officer aboard the *USS Gary* and *USS Boxer.* Earning
his second master's degree in 2012 and during a stint as a duty
engineer in San Diego, Benda would receive his orders for duty
aboard the *USS Constitution.* He is presently the commander of
the *USS Constitution,* the world's oldest commissioned naval
vessel afloat. Benda is a Holliston resident living in the heart of
Mudville on Exchange Street.

Author Bobby Blair, aka "The Mayor of Mudville"

About the Author

Bobby Blair is a homegrown Hollistonian. His paternal side is traced back via DNA to Scotland and Jean Francois, the first Blair of the Blairs, around the year 1190. His maternal ancestors hail from Ireland and settled in Holliston's Mudville neighborhood during the Irish Potato Famine of the 1840s. Bobby served with the Army's First Field Forces, Fifty-second Artillery Group, Seventh Battalion Fifteenth Field Artillery Regiment in An Khe and Pleiku, Vietnam. A past commander for both the local American Legion Post 47 and VFW Post 8507, Blair retired from the Holliston Post Office after thirty-seven years as a letter carrier in 2005.

Blair is known locally as the "Mayor of Mudville," having initiated the first Mudville block party in 1981. He was named a "Holliston Citizen of the Year" in 1997 and *MetroWest Daily News* "Man of the Year" in 2005. In 2005, Blair began writing for Mary Greendale's *Holliston Net News* and several years later formed the *Holliston Reporter* with fellow colleagues Bill Tobin and Paul Saulnier. For the past 15 years, Blair has farmed on Highland Street in Holliston, growing dahlias as a main crop. Combining his interest in writing and veterans affairs, *A Holliston Call to Duty* is an exercise in posterity for future generations.